To Build Up…

Under

Construction

Inspirational Poetry

by

Kevin Boyland

To Build Up… Under Construction: Inspirational Poetry

Copyright © 2024 by Kevin Boyland

ISBN: 979-8-89075-689-3

Dedication

I would like to dedicate this book to my family and anyone needing an encouraging word.

Acknowledgement

I would like to acknowledge Pastor Miller and Pastor Gryzbec who are pictured in the baptism photos at the end of the book.

I would also like to acknowledge Hope City Church where I currently attend and continue to be fed spiritually.

About the Author

Kevin Boyland was born in Memphis, Tennessee. As a child he grew up fishing with his dad and developed a lifelong love for the sport. He, also through his parents, developed a love for cooking, particularly barbequing. Kevin's love for writing began in his junior high school years. He came to accept Jesus Christ into his heart in 2003 and spent most of his life serving.

He is a twenty-year veteran of the military and has retired from twenty-five years of law enforcement. After coming to the Lord, Kevin completed a two-year discipleship course to learn more about God. In seeking that relationship with Jesus, Kevin's poetry reflects testimonies that have been shared with him, his own personal life, and the Word of God that has inspired him. His poetry, he prays, can touch others in the way of edification. Kevin believes that it is easier to tear down than to build up and we as Christians are in a continual process of being constructed through our purpose to serve the will of God.

CONTENTS

Introduction

This collection of poetry has been a labor of love. From a young age I always dabbled in writing and enjoyed it. Throughout life we all face our fair share of ups and downs. Prior to coming to Jesus Christ, life is truly a struggle. Coming to Christ and digging into the Word of God gives our life a true sense of hope in God. Having Jesus as your Savior does not guarantee a carefree life. Without Jesus the struggle is real, however with Him nothing is impossible.

Philippians 4:6-7 (ESV)

Do not be anxious about anything, but in everything by prayer and supplication with thanksgiving let your requests be made known to God. And the peace of God, which surpasses all understanding, will guard your hearts and minds in Christ Jesus.

In The Name Of

Many have come to know Him, and many are yet to find

The Body of Christ is to serve God's will till the end of time

He that conquers, He that rules, He is all that you need

He is known by many names, our intercessor of pleas

We are in a world filled with sin, no circumstance too delicate

He is our Advocate

We are His sheep whom He protects with His staff and thy rod

He is the Good Shepherd, the Son of God

The One who is just, fair, and holds no grudge

Give Him all the honor, Judge

The price paid for man's sins by God's will and His accord

Blessed our King of kings, our Lord of lords

When our faith is weak, He is the door that is never locked

He is our strength, the Rock

He is the key to heaven and knows all that we are

Our Lord and Master

To find redemption, deliverance, and salvation in your search

Seek only the Head of the Church

He who is arisen, whose teaching will never cease

High Priest

Many are caught up in the material world of bling

A focus that is short of our Day Spring

Whenever darkness comes upon you, regardless of where you are

It is He that shines the Bright Morning Star

He is the Word, and the Bible is filled with His Good News

He is the King of the Jews

To never thirst again, give honor, praise and glory to our Father

For He quinches the Living Water

He lights the way for every man, woman, boy, and girl

He is the Light of the World

The list goes on and there is only one in whom you can trust

He that has many names that began with Jesus

All that He has done for man, and He will never quit

All things possible in the name of the Father, the Son, and the Holy Spirit

Chapter 1

Salvation

In this life, there are people who are unbelievers, and then there are people who come to Christ and are now believers. Once becoming a believer there is another step that we must strive for, and that is to become a disciple. Sin entered the world and a fight for our salvation has been ever so present by the love of God for each and every one of us, so that no soul may be lost. Each of us has a purpose that involves loving our fellow man and to be a light to those who are still in the dark.

Luke 1:68-69 (NLT)

Praise the Lord, God of Israel, because he has visited and redeemed his people. He has sent us a mighty Savior from the royal line of his servant David...

The Sin

Ever since Adam and Eve, way back when
Even to this day, the flesh is filled with sin
There's no escaping, for sin is inherent
Either thought or action, it is so apparent

It's a part of our makeup, you can call it DNA
There are no genetic markers, but the price we pay
Beyond the flesh through Christ can one ever be free
Lift the Holy Spirit of the Lord, He is the key

The kingdom awaits with your final breath
Then is one void of sin only through death
Claim your victory now, for the flesh is weak
Gather your strength in the Lord, it is he that you seek

Lost and Found

Once I was a soul that was lost

Who lived in sin that came at a cost

A life where I had very little care

Until no longer could I bear

A friend said one word to me

It was so profound that it changed my destiny

"Jesus", that pierced through my heart

A moment where I received a brand-new start

I found the Lord or was it that He found me

I was lost in wickedness and then set free

I yearn now for the warmth of His light

Heated by truth, love and that which is right

Ever so grateful that Christ is risen

And the Spirit of God no longer hidden

I am that sheep brought into the fold

I am found and my testimony to be told

I now give praise and worship on bended knee

Glory to God, My Savior Jesus, I am not worthy

The Harvest

Our Father creator of heaven and earth

Who is all knowing and knows our worth

Many souls have come before the Lord

Those souls now have a guaranteed reward

The Lambs Book of Life their names written in

Countless souls still lost living in a life of sin

His light has illuminated that path of righteousness

Time is running out on those souls lost in the wilderness

Seek those souls lost and you shall find

Lost souls don't know that they are running out of time

The harvest is upon man and record crops are in the field

Neither rain nor drought can affect the yield

Machine and combines are all out of commission

Help wanted; laborers needed for the mission

Laborers for the Lord, you will find that the harvest is ripe

The field is filled with commodities of every type

Gather as many souls as possible and bring before our King

May the fruit from our labor make the angels dance and sing

Set ablaze the passion for our Father and His Son

Not forsaking the Comforter for we have already won

Our pay day is the kingdom and oh what a thrill

An eternity with our God in service to His will

Soldiers For Christ

There is war going on and the battle has many fronts

Soldiers needed for the crusade are called to be grunts

There is no draft and the call to arms is voluntary

The fight is in the trenches, every saved soldier is necessary

Our objective you will encounter everywhere you go

Lost souls in our midst as well as our foe

Soldiers who have enlisted are commanded by the Lord

You have suited up with His armor and ready to yield His sword

One's faith and belief strengthen your intestinal fortitude

The soldier's manual "a.k.a." the Bible prepares us and serves as food

Train daily with the Word to become proficient in your fight

The battle against darkness will eventually succumb to the Light

Get to know the enemy strengths as well as his weakness

The fight prepared for you is his only form of business

The enemy comes at you one on one or attacks a group of any size

Seeking to steal, kill, destroy and to even paralyze

God almighty only knows when this war will come to an end

Until that moment comes, our Savior and I will defend

Take what the Lord has given and lay it on the line

March right into battle and do not stay idle by just marking time

Chapter 2
Testimonies

History is a time that has passed with a story to be told. The story shared should be information we can learn from and have applications that can be utilized within one's life. The best story ever in my heart is His story. Jesus lived, died, and rose from the dead because of the love God the Father has for His creation "mankind".

The next collection refers to testimonies that I have lived and experienced in my life and have seen in the lives of others. The Word of God knows all that we will face in a lifetime. God's Word is filled with examples of testimonies, and it shows what we must avoid, what we need to apply to our lives and strive to be Christ like. What we share with others is to impart what we have dealt with, how God forged us through the storm and show love to our fellow man. Community is vital to Christian living.

Hebrews 10:24-25 (ESV)

And let us consider how to stir up one another to love and good works, not neglecting to meet together, as is the habit of some, but encouraging one another, and all the more as you see the Day drawing near.

Struggles

Another long and restless night

Fully awakened by the morning light

A brand-new day and on my own

Just figuring out how to get along

I see the bills piled high upon the desk

Time to rob Peter to pay Paul at best

Stretched beyond my means with no relief in sight

Trying to maintain and do what is right

Worry and stress over runneth my cup

Yes, it makes me angry and want to give up

Struggles reaching into every aspect of life

Children, significant other, husband or a wife

As the stress mounts, it begins to take its toll

Resentment in relationships starts to unfold

Two hearts that used to beat as one

Emotions closed off, feelings becoming undone

You look for an answer and willing to take a chance

But the grass is not greener on the other side of the fence

Can you talk to your family or maybe a friend?

Will they truly listen, will they understand?

Can one really know how much that they can really share?

Open and vulnerable, a lot for one to bare

Turmoil in our lives and we will all be tested

And within the Good Book, our answers are vested

Before our life on earth can ever be whole

Speak with thy lips and give Jesus your soul

Search your heart and work to make amends

Gather Christian support of family and friends

And do not expect miracles to happen overnight

It is by God's will that the timing will be right

The day will come, and your soul will soar

Blessings from our Savior, whose love you cannot ignore

Place the Lord first and surely you will find

All things possible, no struggles to bind

Fade From Dark to Light

I walk through life, and I have not received the Lord

I believe in God, that is all that I can afford

I am not a church goer, that life is not for me

I am living my life, what more can there be

I do things acceptable in the eyes of society today

The things not acceptable, for that a time or two I did pray

I am living my life and often the things that I have done

I have done for so long that now I have become numb

My conscience, No! Mine does not bother me

I have reasoned and justified through my eyes in which I see

I have gone to church, and I really do believe in God

Halfway through the service, my eyes are heavy, and I would nod

Something I found not to be all that great

Was the money I had to put in that collection plate

I look around the congregation just to see

Who is wearing what, and who is looking down on me

A holiday comes around and I am back in church at last

I have missed a month of Sundays, my how time has passed

The times I have listened to the message, was it just for me

I would feel uncomfortable, I am here today, just let me be

I would receive the Lord, but what would that mean

The transformation in others I have seen

What would my friends think or say

To know that I am committed to church on Sundays

What is this gut feeling that seems to arise

When thoughts of past practices no longer in disguise

I see things differently in my heart and mind

I look back now and wish that I could rewind

Rewind to a time before I went down the wrong road

Now my sight is set on Jesus, I will reap what I have sown

I cannot explain and it is all too strange

As my shell is the same, but the inner me, totally
rearranged

I can go now and give my soul to the Lord

I have taken the sin in my life and severed the umbilical
cord

Whatever circumstance that brings forth Jesus for a soul to
know

Care must be taken that the seed planted has a chance to
grow

Once a soul is touched, there will be mixed feelings

Know that the presence of the Lord has begun His healing

Leave It at The Altar

The Blood of the Lamb can wash away sin

Salvation our greatest attainment once born again

The power of God in Jesus reigns supreme

The gift of love for every human being

Once you have given your heart to the Lord

Change your life for God's will by your accord

The power of God can no man conceive

Which demands faith and to believe

You come before the altar to turn everything in

All your past, every sin

You repent, praise and leave those burdens behind

And at times, you will question it in your mind

When on the altar, there was no doubt

Born again in Jesus' name and the Holy Spirit was about

The mind cannot conceive but you made the call

Listen now to your heart which will reveal it all

You asked to be forgiven which the Lord has done

Take forth the fruit and share, for you have already won

I Am Not Worthy

How can you thank Jesus who is pure love

How can you thank our Father on His throne above

How can you thank Jesus for His crown of thorns

How can you thank Jesus that you can be reborn

How can you thank Jesus who was crucified

How can you thank Jesus for the reason He died

How can you thank Jesus for answering prayers

How can you thank the One who really cares

How can you thank Jesus who is all true

How can you thank the One who will never forsake you

How can you thank Jesus who sees in the heart

How can you thank Jesus who was there from the start

How can you thank God for Jesus who is risen

How can you show thanks, take a moment and listen

Thank you, God, for all that you have given

Thank you, Lord, for my reason to be living

I worship you with all my might

I worship you that is my true Light

I praise you Lord and Savior on high

I praise my Lord and Savior, hear my cry

I give you all the honor as well as the glory

Allow me to bestow it all upon thee

I strive to obey Your will and always tithe

May my actions show, by this I abide

I could never give all the thanks that You are due

But my heart is filled with my love for You

Renewed Strength

Lord come into my life and throw away the key

No longer will I separate You from me

You have always been there, even when I have not

Yet You have accepted me back without a second thought

I am now that new creation who is born again

And You never gave up on me, what a true friend

The path that I was on and the life that I had led

Is one of no more, one that I am glad to say is dead

I pray to you Lord that I always stay on track

My past a distant memory, no longer will I go back

Give me strength so that I may endure

Your love and grace are my cure

My soul belongs to You, and I now stand firm

I get into the word so that I may learn

My Lord and Savior, you are one of a kind

I love you with my entire heart, soul, and mind

I prepared my heart now so that I may receive

For no longer will I question, for I have faith and believe

A Ripple in the Water

It does not matter the hour when the call comes in

There is disbelief and shock that affect family and friends

A person's life has impact on all that they knew

So, news of a traumatic event stretches beyond just a few

Tragedies that make us all so furious

It could never happen to us, it's to ridiculous

The ripple no matter how big or small

Continuous from the center and reaches one and all

The blow hits home the hardest at first

Sympathies for the family, for their grief is the worst

Friends also taken aback in disbelief

A moment to reflect as we all share in the grief

The ripple will continue until the surface is smooth

They say that with time our hearts will improve

We will always wonder what went wrong

Coping with the fact that a loved one is really gone

From this moment on, we must begin anew

You are treasured in our memories and forever we'll miss you

May the Lord ease our pain and help us to deal

As we say goodbye and take time to heal

You are in our hearts, and we will never forget

To lose you now is our greatest regret

Recognize the Signs

There is no way to conceive but I do believe

Miracles, signs, and wonders only our God can achieve

We are all given a purpose here on this earth

Which will prove to be a testimony of our worth

There is no greater love, for Jesus paid the ultimate cost

Many lives we will encounter, some saved, some lost

We are guided by our Savior who shines ever so bright

He sees into our hearts and brings the dark to light

Miracles always happening and seen with the naked eye

Some question it in their mind, but the heart cannot deny

Signs and wonders are evident, just look and you will see

Some so subtly, you will ask how this can be

A husband and wife taken by an act of violence

Family and friends at the burial and in a moment of silence

Lo! and behold for the family to see

Two butterflies fluttering in the wind, free as can be

An awesome moment in the time of grief

Heaviness lifted in the heart and a sigh of relief

There is good trapped in darkness that we may not always see

But Jesus is the Light and His grace and love is the key

Trust in the Lord, for Jesus is the way

Glorify and honor when you sing and pray

So, when it defies your logic and you sit and ponder

Know that it is the King of kings, His miracles, signs and wonders

Chapter 3

Trinity

The saying "all for one and one for all" seems to be so appropriate. Here we have three distinct persons whose love for mankind exceeds our understanding. As we are the creation of God the Father who gave us Jesus, God the Son, who paid the price for our sins and made available to us a Comforter, God the Holy Spirit, who convicts us of righteousness.

A personal relationship with the Lord our God is what we all need on this side of heaven. This relationship comes through reading the Word of God, getting equipped for service through church attendance, building a community of likeminded believers, and sharing the love of God with those in your sphere of influence.

Mark 12:30 (ESV)

And you shall love the Lord your God with all your heart and with all your soul and with all your mind and with all your strength.

I Am

I Am the creator of heaven and earth who is above all

I Am the provider for all creatures great and small

I Am the One who gives out of the abundance of My heart with joy

I Am that I do willingly for every man, woman, girl, and boy

I Am the fortress in which your foundation is built

I Am that Jesus came to cleanse all from sin and guilt

I Am the missing link whose compassion makes you complete

I Am that your walk in Christ may shine upon those you meet

When you are troubled and at a time filled with fear

I Am the peace that you seek and know that I Am always near

Know that anything formed against you shall not be able to stand

For I Am more formidable than any principality, darkness or man

Forget not my benefits in which I promised to share

I Am your God and my Son I have given as a sign of my care

I Am the Word and the Word was made flesh through Jesus Christ

I Am that Christ conquered death, so that you may have life

I Am here, there, and everywhere so that no man may boast

I Am the Comforter; I Am the Spirit that fills you with the Holy Ghost

I Am your companion who is there wherever you go

In your heart I dwell, my Word is true, this you know that you know

I Am that My Word is the first and last authority

I Am the Gospel, make the Great Commission your priority

I Am the Light that radiates the earth, heaven, and into eternity

I Am the door, open to salvation, the impossible set free

I Am the Father who disciplines, who holds you accountable for your debts

I Am the One who also forgives and the Father who forgets

I Am that I Am, which defies limitations when it comes to you

Give Me your heart, praise, and worship, for I long to have you too.

Looking for Jesus

Far too long many souls have been blind

Their eyes are open and cannot find

Find the face that is meant for thee

To find the face that can set you free

Those that have sought and created such a fuss

Already know that the face belongs to Jesus

To look upon the greatness that God gave

Can only come by way of being saved

This is not a game of hide and seek

It does not matter whether you are strong or weak

There is no favor whether you are rich or poor

Save your soul so that you may endure

Jesus is the Light that can show you the way

A life of fulfillment, to keep the dark at bay

Jesus brought forth a promise for all of man

In that hour of need, Jesus provides that helping hand

Our Redeemer is quite easy to find

Just open your heart, soul, and mind

Use every ounce of your power and might

To receive your salvation from the Light

To our Father give praise, honor, and glory

Give thanks for the deliverance and one less worry

The Spirit Within Me

I never knew that the day would come

When my life changed, completely undone

With the Word of God and touched for the very first time

A movement within my soul, so incredible, yet utterly divine

An awakening like nothing ever before

Floods of emotions as my souls starts to soar

A feeling of weakness about my knees

Wishing only for the Lord to please

No longer can I see for the tears in my eyes

A cleansing, a deliverance as I cry

I am now that sheep gathered into the flock

My stronghold the Lord, solid as a rock

Overwhelmed with all that I feel

Now living by God's Word as my will

Minister now to all that will hear me

Sharing God's Word and take charge of my destiny

The Spirit is within me

I Love You

I cannot be, if not for thee

Lasting into eternity
Only you and me
Venturing life together
Even through stormy weather

Just, fair, impartial, and pure
Everything that man should strive to secure
Spiritually One with the Father and I with thee
Unending truth and hope for all to see
Savior of anyone that chose to be free

Call on the Lord and He will call on you
His mercy and grace can see you through
Reaching as many souls as times ticks away
Instilling God's Word, listen and hear Him say
Salvation is yours, you need only to ask
The kingdom awaits, the last to be first, the first to be last

Predetermined

Before our first breath, even before the moment of conception

A predetermined plan has been conceived, awaiting our inception

There are no mistakes that surrounds our date of birth

Only our Father knows our purpose and our worth

Some may or may not even know or conceive

What their role is in life or how to receive

How to receive the Lord as a personal Savior

Once accepted His love changes ones' behavior

Jesus is and will always be the lover of our soul

He has released a new creation, one that is now in control

Now look and clearly see our purpose in whom we serve

Our free will to serve His will, His grace we don't deserve

Every day we should die and surrender to You

Grant us the knowledge to fulfill that You would have us to do

It is not about us, far greater is our heavenly Father above

He desires our gifts, every form of worship and unconditional love

Our time here on earth is merely a steppingstone

Release your heart, soul, strength, and mind before His throne

His eternal vision through our eyes we will never see

Only through our heart and Jesus can heaven ever be

He Is

He is my walk that steps towards righteousness

This is the walk that I yearn to achieve with success

He is my speech for every soul that I reach

May my voice carry His word so that I may teach

He is my eyes that can see the future

As I look, I am confident and sure

He is my heart that beats for the Blood of the Lamb

My life force that drives who I am

He is my strength that powers over me

That lifted the weight and has set me free

He is my friend who will always be there

To go without, a thought that I cannot bear

He is my peace that is there when I yield

He gives me the comfort that I long to feel

He is my light, let no darkness overshadow me

The path of righteousness shines for all to see

He is my King whom I gladly serve

Who cleansed my sins that I do not deserve

He is my Savior who blesses beyond the curse

Plant the Word in your heart, verse by verse

He is my Lord whom I worship and praise

He who is worthy of all honor and glory in these final days

He is my spirit that fills me up

There is never enough, please over runneth my cup

He is that He is and you know that you know

Jesus Christ our Savior, He is there wherever you go

Power of Prayer

Father, give ear to this prayer as we call unto You

By your power and grace, we shall make it through

Here is a soul that humbly needs to be in your favor

As we pray for mercy and grace from our Savior

Stricken by a condition in this physical realm

This soul prays that the Comforter is at the helm

We gather and strengthen our love for our fellow man

As we stretch and lay forth our hands

We lift up thy name that charges over healing

As we pray to rid this ailment that one is enduring

Thine miracles, signs and wonders only You possess

Given Your timetable we pray that you bless

Bless this soul who must surely yield

Yield to the Holy Spirit whom we pray will heal

Hear us Father as we pray in the name of Your Son

Through Christ Jesus can Your will be done

The Whisper

What is this whisper that I hear in my ear

So soft and gently as I draw to have it near

My imagination, no that cannot be

The word spoken meant just for me

The love in my heart that flows like that of a flood

My heart pounds with joy, for the Spirit is fully understood

My entire existence ceases to exist

As my head clouds and my eyes begin to mist

Holding on and swayed by the purity within

Thankful for what the Holy Spirit has given

And forevermore shall I hold dear

What was whispered in my ear

The Cross Built for Mankind

It was foreseen and foretold

Ever since the days of old

There was talk of a certain birth

A child of God that blessed this earth

Jesus went to Jordan and was baptized by John

From that moment forward, His ministry begun

Tempted by Satan was He

Temptation that never came to be

The multitudes came and dwelled

Jesus enlisted His disciples of twelve

They were sent with the Word they were given

They became fishers of men

Jesus worked miracles by His hand

Five loaves, two fish, He feeds five thousand

Jesus, healed, ministered and then was betrayed

Of the twelve, one strayed

Strayed for thirty pieces of silver

For that Judas would deliver

Jesus was taken to Calvary

Where He died for thee

Crucified and shed His blood upon the cross

Agape love paid the ultimate cost

One, two, three days have passed

Christ Jesus risen at last

Now at the right hand of our Father

Now our redeemer who can only deliver

A kingdom in heaven prepared for us all

For those who have sought and made the call

Coming of the King

When our Savior returns, no one will see

Unexpected the day Jesus comes for thee

A tidal wave of love for those souls that prepared

My heart goes out to those souls that dared

For the Kingdom of God is promised to us all

Make your house right or face a certain fall

There is nowhere to run, there is nowhere to hide

And the coming of the Lord has been prophesied

Plant the Word deep within your spirit

Strengthen your soul and deny the false prophets

Watch for the peace that enters the land

The calm before the storm will be upon man

We are now living in that time and the future is unsure

May salvation in your heart be honest and pure

When deliverance is at hand, may your soul endure

For the souls still lost, Jesus is the cure

Chapter 4

Witnessing

Coming to know Jesus in a personal relationship is an important element of being a Christian. Everything that we as people go through that God brought us out of is a statement of who He is. He loved us first and that is a love that will never end. The trials and tribulations that we have endured through God's grace and mercy make us a witness to others to show the love of God that we can impart to others who face situations and feel that there is no hope. Our vertical relationship with God is as vital as the relationship we have horizontally with our fellow man. Thus, we must share the Gospel of Christ.

Acts 1:8 (ESV)

But you will receive power when the Holy Spirit has come upon you, and you will be my witnesses in Jerusalem and in all Judea and Samaria, and to the ends of the earth.

Movies to Move You

I asked for Jesus as my Savior and He came without hesitation

This soul, which was once lost, now has a **Final Destination**

For me to serve God's will and become all that I am

Requires spreading of the Gospel, no **Silence of the Lamb**

We enter this world striving to be all that we can be

Fighting the flesh, the world and Satan, defining **The Good, The Bad and The Ugly**

We are given the Word of God, and listen as the Holy Spirit beckons

For life is too short and can be **Gone in 60 Seconds**

The Word of God is our foundation and serves us with all truth

Some change like Clark Kent into **Superman**, using a **Phone Booth**

And yes, before the Blood, our lives are like a **Scary Movie**

And blessed are those to receive Jesus and a new **Bourne Identity**

To walk with the Lord, you will find that your life is truly full

As we strive to serve others, no **Mission Impossible**

Our walk will have its trials and we will do some crying

Our joy comes from reaching souls, like **Saving Private Ryan**

In our quest for souls, we will encounter a multitude of sin

That is why it takes the whole body, and not just **A Few Good Men**

There are many temptations that each of us will encounter

The only place to turn for our strength is our **Master and Commander**

So, keep in mind one thing with every soul that you meet

Have they seen the Light or caught in a bad dream, like a **Nightmare on Elm Street**

Soul Searching

Together let us imagine how houses are like souls

Some are new, some are old, each with a story to be told

Some are rich, others are moderate, and some are poor

Some stood the test of time and still endure

Imagine houses with nice lawns, others with shrubs and overgrown

Some of you would feel welcoming, others you would leave alone

Some houses have many windows, others with just a few

Some are appealing and some without a view

Some of those windows have curtains or blinds

Some you cannot see into, while others do not mind

Look inside the house, it may be kept or in disarray

Every house needs cleaning every day

Each house is unique and has a certain style

Most are inhabited, some vacant for a while

Each room in a house serves a specific need

Houses are owned or rented, who controls your deed

All houses need maintenance, that's a sure bet

Nothing to be neglected, to include the closet

Houses come in a variety of colors, construction varies too

Each home should serve the same purpose whether old or new

There are homes that are destroyed by fire

What a shame to see any home expire

Some houses are condemned and demolished to the ground

Some get rebuilt and others an eyesore around town

Much is vested, insure the house and the property within

Just in case of trouble, have the insurance you can depend

Every day houses are purchased and put up for sale

Take root of your homestead, do it without fail

To turn a house into a home

Fill it with the Lord and you cannot go wrong

So, when does a house finally become a home

When the love from the inside out can be shown

Opportunity

Each day we are given an incredible chance

One to make the angels in heaven to sing and dance

The morning sun rises out of the east and sets in the west

Every waking moment we are put to the test

We will encounter family, friends, and strangers as well

Each with the potential to bring us out of our shell

We have given our life to the Lord, which is not enough

The thought of sharing with others can prove to be tough

We hope that everyone will come to know

That Jesus is our Savior, which we must show

We go to get groceries at any store

In every aisle is a chance to score

We go to the movies to see a show

Surrounded by souls we do not even know

We stop at the service station and fill up with gas

You ever wonder how many lost souls you have passed

We all attend school, each to a certain level

How many are with God, versus those with the Devil

Hiking, camping, fishing any hobby that you do

Also shared by lost souls right next to you

Next door, across the street, up and down the block

How many neighbors are there, not a part of the flock

Lost souls attend church, they are in the right place

They just haven't submitted and relinquished to God's grace

Many will say, how do I begin such a task

My brothers and sisters, I am glad that you asked

The door can be opened in many different ways

So, there is no standard response as to what to say

Where you worship can be a very good start

A chance to open the door and a glimpse into their heart

Mentally prepare for the responses you will receive

Have faith in the Lord, because not all will believe

You may be nervous, anxious and possibly tongue tied

Scared or awkward, but know that Jesus is by your side

And with each soul, may a seed fall upon them

Each experience will bless you, let no soul be condemned

We are all apt to talk the talk

But reserved when it is time to walk the walk

The Lord gives us just what we need

Listen now to your heart and please take heed

We have been given salvation, we have been freed

The love for mankind is how we will succeed

So, let us go forth to plant, water, or harvest the seed

And stand in judgement by our deeds

Be the Church

Certain tastes appeal to one during their search

When looking to find just the right church

Once it is found, you can now call home

Surrounded by the same beliefs, just as your own

You are there to give praise and worship on Sunday morn

Thankful for your salvation, blessed to be reborn

Sunday service came and went

You choose not to attend, and several are absent

You begin a brand-new week, back at the same old grind

You make it to hump day and say it is about time

Wednesday night Bible study, you are too busy or just tired

A few days without the Word and you are not inspired

Your Bible lay dormant all week long

You say your prayers and feel nothing more is wrong

Another week down and it is Sunday once again

You come before the One in which you know that you can depend

Some routines for worship come only once a week

Charged up on Sunday morning with nothing more to seek

Then you are faced with a situation beyond your control

You call on the One who has saved your soul

He is always there for you, despite the standards you have set

For Jesus will never forsake you, you will always be in His debt

There are many ways we can try to repay

Attend services and get into the Word everyday

Reach out to others and share what the Lord has said

Make this your standard routine, as your daily bread

None of us are perfect and should strive to do our best

To find favor with the Lord, give more, not less

Inside the Bottle

The first sip no longer can I remember

A time of discovery for that taste that would deliver

Straight down the hatch and into the bloodstream

The head gets light, what does this feeling mean

There is beer, wine, and of course hard liquor

Underage or not, the hard liquor works quicker

A level head, then a buzz, and now drunk

It went down so smooth, what a slam dunk

Before the alcohol and after it takes effect

Compares to Dr. Jekyll and Mr. Hyde in respect

Once quiet and shy, now loud and bold

Loss of inhibitions, take chances and loss of control

The depressant that brought you up will bring you down

Hang over, dry heaves, face and toilet, both are bound

Some drink before they reach that magical age

Some need a drink to perform on the social stage

Some will find that the bottle is their only friend

The bottle does not judge, a crutch that one will depend

The drink may provoke meanness and one to fight

It becomes a way of life, it becomes ones' plight

All too often there is a reason to get drunk and forget

And the moment of sobriety brings back the memories and the regret

And over time the body decides to take a stance

It requires more alcohol to create a new tolerance

Drink to a point when one is totally numb

Blood alcohol level like a steak, well done

Effects reach beyond you, family, and work

Loss of trust, bad credit, closet drinker, where is the perk

The poison ingested comes at what cost

Public intoxication, drunk driving, heaven forbid a life lost

Eventually one will hit rock bottom

A time in life, one can never ever fathom

There is only one place to go and that is up

A realization that inside the bottle is corrupt

You look into the mirror and what do you find

Recovery is done one day at a time

Also release your heart to the ultimate power

Jesus can see you through it, hour by hour

His power, grace, and love, make it a part of your will

For the Lord can deliver as well as heal

Jesus is My Answer

It starts with the very first smoke

You light it, you gag, and you choke

You continue until the very end

Not realizing how the chemicals will become your friend

Before long you decide to buy that pack

Not knowing how it will become that monkey on your back

There are the menthols, non-menthols, kings, and the longs

You decide on a favorite brand as the addiction becomes strong

You get a cigarette and once it is lit

It is a part of your life, now it has become a habit

You think that you are immune because the damage is inside

You know your lungs are struggling as they get fried

You fool yourself and say that it is no big deal

But in the same breath, you note how you feel

You go for a while without a care

You start to feel the effects and occasionally gasp for air

Then you decide it is time to quit

But the nicotine cravings give you a fit

Cold turkey does not seem to work

The withdrawal symptoms do not pose to be a perk

Then I try the pill, the gum, and the patch

And for some reason, none of them seem to be a match

So, I try and most often fail

Then I wonder if one can prevail

Then it dons on me where to find the answer

And by God's will, hopefully there is no cancer

So, I look to the Lord to get an answer for me

And I pray that I can be smoke free

Oblivious to the answer for so long

No wonder all that I tried was always wrong

Now I see that it is all too simple

As I began to cleanse God's temple

My flesh is on loan here on this earth

And only the Lord knows my true worth

So, I put this addiction in the Lord's hand

That I may grow spiritually and become free again.

Ministry

Every living soul on this earth is unique in their own way

From the moment we enter this world, life molds us each day

The path chosen will be smooth and at times can be rough

The trails that do not kill us, will surely make us tough

We as flesh choose moments or a lifetime of sin

Every tribulation conquered makes us a witness so others may win

Everyone is gifted and has a purpose in God's perfect plan

Gifts come in various forms and should serve our fellow man

Ministry is God's glory and spiritual maturity is not self-serving

Use testimonies and witnessing to lead souls to our King

Laborers, the Great Commission is commanded from on high

We are the body and every part that makes the whole must edify

We are all ministers, either active or idle with a gift

Your service can reach others and provide just the right lift

The blood gives us freedom, but life is in Christ's Resurrection

We must evangelize our world and seek other nations

And he who serves, serves God's will and we are His slaves

Our Master provides for His people, for us Christ Jesus He gave

Those of the way, may the fruit of our labor shine

We are living in the last days, let us make the most of our time

Addicted

I have this addiction, let it never ever cease

He is my Savior, the Prince of Peace

I am that junky and cannot get enough

Withdrawal from the Lord would surely be tough

This is a high, there is no higher

The Lord my addiction, a rush I desire

And throughout the day when I am looking for a fix

I feed on His Word just to get a kick

Show me a wagon and no doubt I will fall

Intoxicating the Holy Spirit, give my pusher a call

So, take a look, I may look strung out

I am hooked on Jesus without a doubt

Whatever the price, I am willing to pay

To be of the chosen come judgement day

Whatever the issue that has you at odds

Relinquish to Jesus and give glory to God

There is no soul that cannot afford

My drug the Lord

References

Philippians 4:6,7 ESV

Luke 1:68,69 NLT

Hebrews 10:24,25 ESV

Mark 12:30 ESV

Acts 1:8 ESV